See It Grow

PINE TREE

by Avery Elizabeth Hurt

Consultant: Karen C. Hall, PhD
Botanist
Eugene, Oregon

BEARPORT PUBLISHING

New York, New York

Credits

Cover, © Maria Janicki/Alamy, © Lynda Lehmann/Shutterstock, and © Tom Grundy/Shutterstock; Title Page, © Billion Photos/Shutterstock; TOC, © Mike Cavaroc/Alamy; 4–5, © DNY59/iStock and © Jill Shepherd/Shutterstock; 6, © NatPar Collection/Alamy; 7, © kemper71/Shutterstock and © ifong/Shutterstock; 8, © kemper71/Shutterstock and © ifong/Shutterstock; 9T, © kemper71/Shutterstock; 9B, © kemper71/Shutterstock; 10, © David R. Frazier/Science Source; 11, © Pro2sound/iStock; 12, © Doug Wilson/Alamy; 13, © Steve Heap/Shutterstock; 14–15, © Gerald & Buff Corsi/Visuals Unlimited; 16, © Robert J. Erwin/Science Source; 17, © George Ostertag/Alamy; 18, © Buddy Mays/Alamy; 19, © Jim Zipp/Science Source; 20T, © William Harlow/Science Source; 20–21, © Tristan Brynildsen/Shutterstock; 22, © werny/Shutterstock; 23 (T to B), © Romija/Shutterstock, © Proshkin Aleksandr/Shutterstock, © Anakeseenadee/Dreamstime, © funnyangel/Shutterstock, and © kemper71/Shutterstock.

Publisher: Kenn Goin
Senior Editor: Joyce Tavolacci
Creative Director: Spencer Brinker
Design: Debrah Kaiser
Photo Researcher: Thomas Persano

Library of Congress Cataloging-in-Publication Data

Names: Hurt, Avery, author.
Title: Pine tree / by Avery Elizabeth Hurt.
Description: New York, New York : Bearport Publishing Company, 2019. | Series: See it grow | Includes bibliographic references and index.
Identifiers: LCCN 2018009275 (print) | LCCN 2018011407 (ebook) | ISBN 9781684027217 (ebook) | ISBN 9781684026753 (library)
Subjects: LCSH: Pine—Juvenile literature.
Classification: LCC SD397.P55 (ebook) | LCC SD397.P55 H86 2018 (print) | DDC 634.9/751—dc23
LC record available at https://lccn.loc.gov/2018009275

For more information, write to Bearport Publishing Company, Inc., 45 West 21st Street, Suite 3B, New York, New York 10010. Printed in the United States of America.

10 9 8 7 6 5 4 3 2 1

Contents

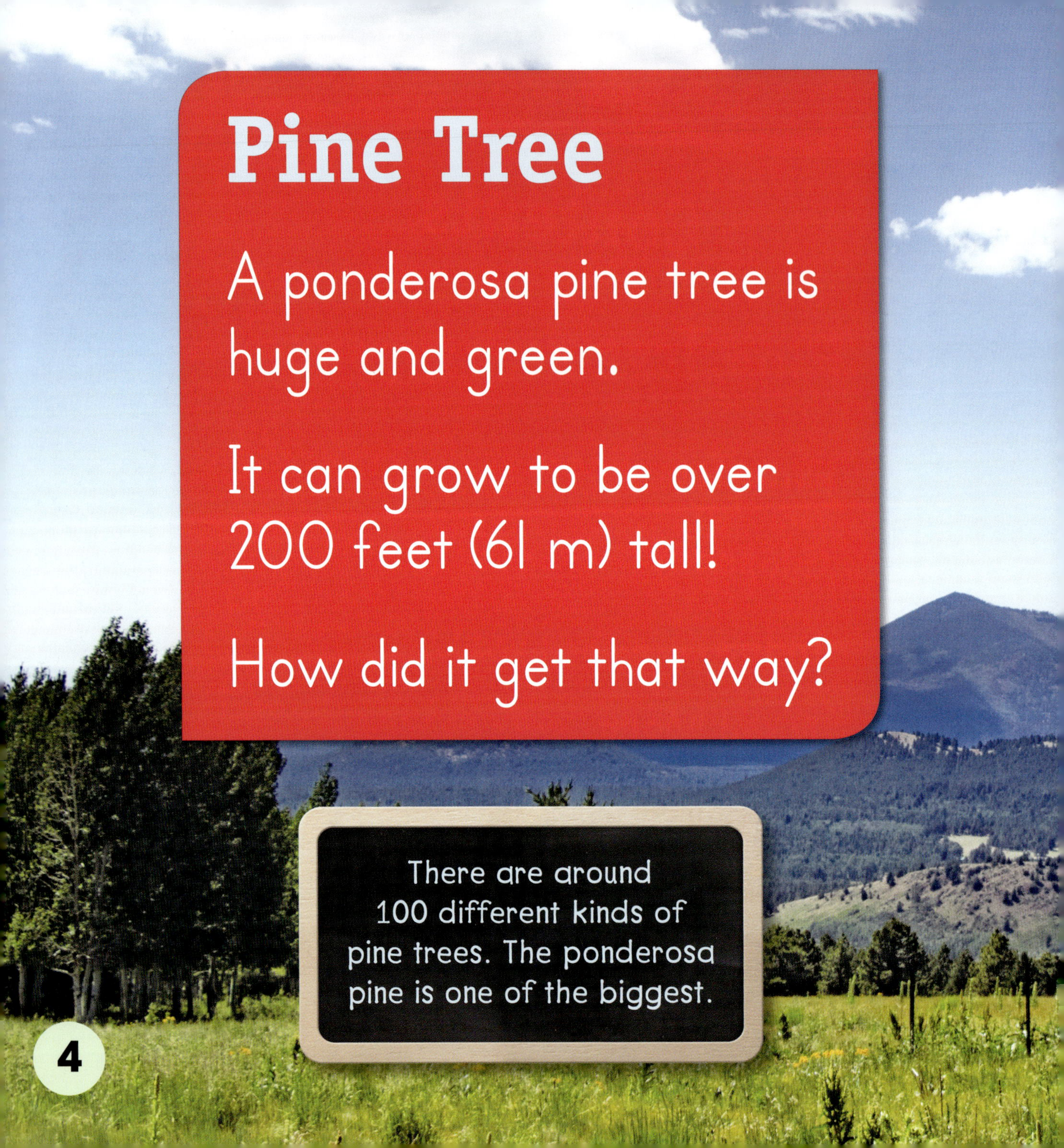

Pine Tree

A ponderosa pine tree is huge and green.

It can grow to be over 200 feet (61 m) tall!

How did it get that way?

There are around 100 different kinds of pine trees. The ponderosa pine is one of the biggest.

A ponderosa pine tree starts out as a tiny seed.

Some kinds of pine seeds can be eaten. They are called pine nuts.

Water and sunlight help the seed grow.

First, the seed sends out little roots into the **soil**.

Then, a tiny **seedling** pops up out of the ground.

It grows and grows.

Next, the little seedling grows leaves.

They're thin and pointy.

Pine tree leaves are called needles.

Pines stay green and don't lose their needles in winter. That's why they're known as evergreens.

The seedling gets bigger.

More needles grow.

The little tree looks like a clump of grass.

Over time, the tree's **stem** turns brown and woody.

The young pine is now a **sapling**.

A tree's hard stem is called a trunk.

Year after year, the sapling grows taller.

Its trunk gets thicker.

Many branches grow out of the trunk.

The trunk is covered with a thick outer layer called bark.

bark

Over time, pine cones grow on the tree's branches.

There are male and female pine cones.

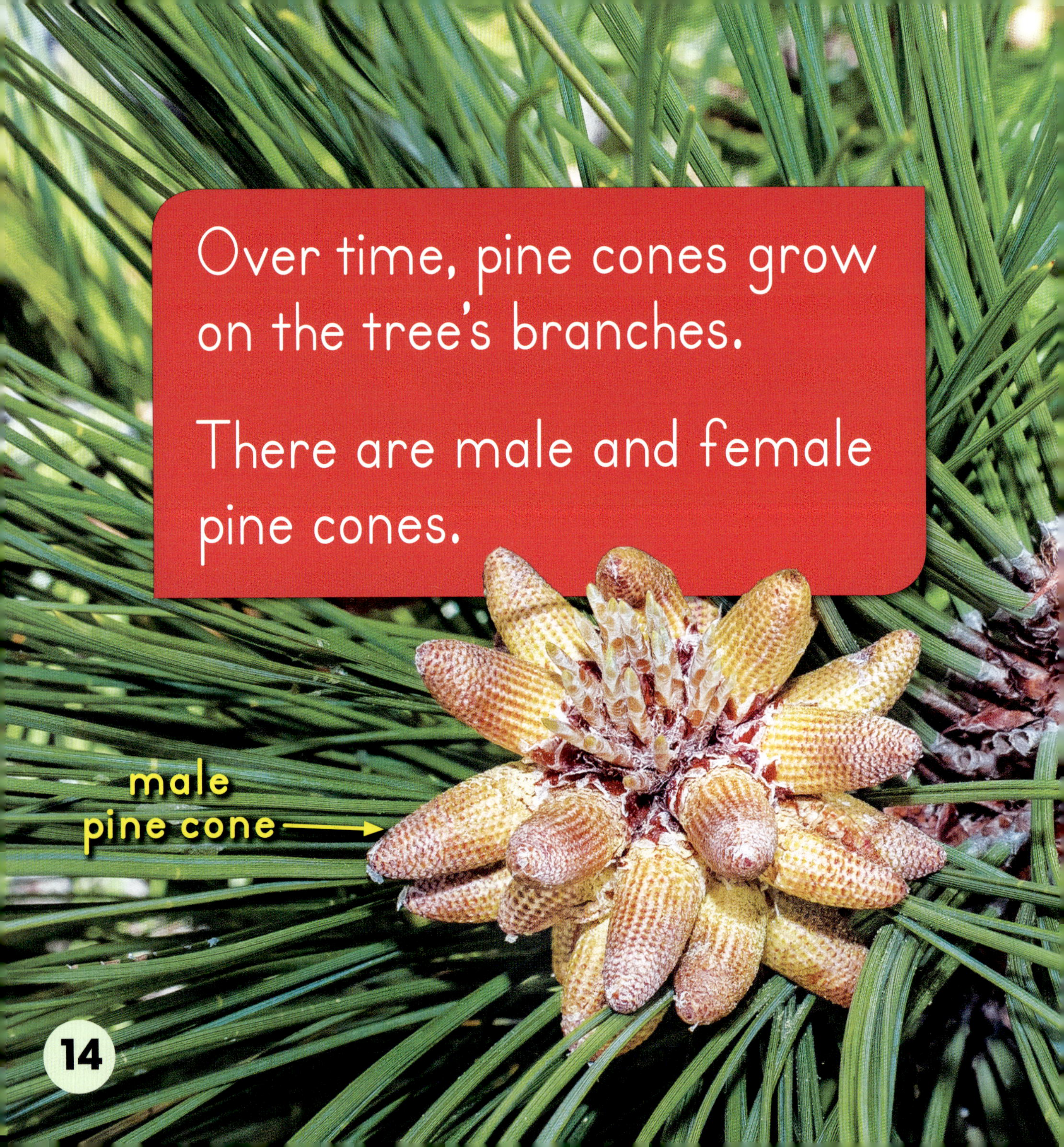

Male pine cones can be yellow or dark red. Female pine cones can be green or dark brown.

The male cones make **pollen.**

Wind blows the pollen to the female cones.

Pine tree pollen looks like a puff of dust.

Then, the female pine cones begin to make seeds.

Seeds develop deep inside a female pine cone.

As the seeds grow, the pine cone gets dry and scaly.

Finally, the scales open up.

After the scales open, birds and other animals feed on the seeds inside.

Some seeds fall out of the pine cone.

They land on the ground.

Soon, a new tree starts to grow.

In many years, it will become a giant pine tree!

Ponderosa pines can live to be 600 years old—or more!

Pine Tree Facts

- Pine trees are used to make paper. In fact, this book was made from a pine tree!
- Many types of pine trees are used for Christmas trees.
- Pine trees store water in their needles.
- Bristlecone pines can live up to 4,500 years!
- When ponderosa pines get old, their bark smells like cookies.

Glossary

pollen (POL-uhn) the fine, yellow dust plants use to make new plants

sapling (SAP-ling) a young tree

seedling (SEED-ling) a very young plant that has grown from a seed

soil (SOYL) the upper layer of earth, where plants grow

stem (STEM) the upright part of a plant that connects the roots to the leaves and flowers

Index

Read More

Berne, Emma Carlson. *From Cone to Pine Tree.* Minneapolis, MN: Lerner (2017).

Blomgren, Jennifer. *Where Would I Be in an Evergreen Tree?* Seattle, WA: Little Bigfoot (2011).

Learn More Online

To learn more about pine trees, visit
www.bearportpublishing.com/SeeItGrow

About the Author

Avery Elizabeth Hurt writes books for young readers. She loves trees of all kinds. She enjoys watching woodpeckers in the dead pine tree behind her house.